We Swallow Light

Copyright © 2022 Tree Langdon

All rights reserved.

First Edition

ISBN: 978-1-7750785-1-7

We Swallow Light

For Danny

You've always had my heart.

I'd like to thank my friends, both online, and in real life for their presence here.

You inspire me with insightful ideas and conversations and I appreciate the support and love you bring into our lives.

I'd also like to thank the difficult people and experiences I've had.

If it weren't for you, I wouldn't have gained the deep knowledge needed to become who I am today.

Contents

This poetry will take you on a journey through events in past lifetimes and relate them to today.

It's a refreshing exploration of overcoming pain and the joy of finding love.

The Binding

Braving The Fire

Rainspears pierce
the thickening clouds.
They bring a heavy darkness
to the dawn.

Towers stand in witness
as the city's Watch
patrols the streets below.

Water swirls in eddies
and flows in concrete riverbeds
rushing as it gathers force.
The liquid is the only traffic
merging in the quiet streets.

Standing on the doorstep
I survey the scene
in quiet contemplation.

Thoughts line up
like strings in rows
that intersect
in unexpected modes.

The monkey mind
sends greetings.
My teeth grind
like marbles
ruffling the tiny hairs
on my neck.

Fear resists the service.
The silence of the streets
unnerves me.

I repeat reminders:
rehearse the mantra.
Take care.
Protect yourself.
Stay back.
Survive.

Bound by duty
I gird my loins.
My focus shifts.
It's time to tie the mask.
I take a breath
and step onto the field.

❖

Rebellion Ignites

It permeates the deepest woods;
an echo of the ancient cry
sent to rally forth the troops.

We link the chains across the land
as runners bring us messages
a marathon has taken place.

A call is carried on the wind;
the whisper of the dissident
expelled in softly puffing breaths.

Now we come upon the choice.
No time for mental wobbling.

When we refuse to speak our truth
and you refuse to hear my heart
we stand between the fragile glass
upon the stone that grinds the sand.

Denial echoes in the woods
and we a herd of sheep ashamed
to gaze upon the truth revealed.

When we listen to the clues
and hear the teeth
as traps spring shut.

We leap.
In an impulse of consideration
we are a single heart and mind.

When the wise ones hear the call
that triggers pictures held beneath
the floorboards of their memories
where tiny bones of field mice
are buried deep within the cells.

Their subversive cross stitch
Shows us where to dig our trench
And how to plant the rebel flag.

It's written in the fragile threads
And etched within the warp and weft
the mantle of a lantern floats.

A magazine and gasoline
Ignites
Time suspended
all direction ends.

❖

Slowly Dying Of Survival

Illusions
in the mote of my eye
are suspended in
the moments of the artistry
that knows the forces
etched in lines upon my face.

They act on every life
beyond my control.
Insight brings the flashes
that surprise our very being
with the lost combination
of the shopping naked feeling

and when you use
your outside voice
to call for clarity
and you realize
you are slowly dying
of survival.

❖

Free Will Was Her Bond

She comes beyond the centuries
Was held within her offered word
She saw the only road to take
A twining, winding, twisting net.

Obscured by words of disbelief
She was compelled to keep the peace.
Free will was given as her bond
Exchanged but for a single life.

Intention freely given once
But bound and taken for all time
Witnessed by the mated twelve
Their fates enlaced infinity.

The lie wrapped in a healing truth
A bargain sealed with binding words.
A soul compelled to give each life
Kept seeking freedom quietly

Invisible, yet powerful
Sustained the simmering disbelief

She kept the search for knots untied
While working for the slow release

A puzzle to be pondered long
To find the clue that was the key
The words to speak to open doors
Until a trail of breadcrumbs left

A meeting with a healing force
Who saw the wrapping wound around
And gave the key to twist the ropes
The words to change the bindings course.

To clear with ritual and intent
Magnifies a light each day
The words to rouse the guardians.
The keepers of the records heard.

They loosed the bindings from her soul
She finds the fullness of her force
And heals the injured web surround
Then steps beyond the absolute

For she is now no longer bound.

Who's Behind the Mask

I stumbled over words
as I struggled
to hold
the mask of character
firmly in its place.

My persona tripped
on ballerina legs
tipped with
impossible heels,

and I dripped
with fascinators
chosen by another.

My quiet anger
was excited
by the private wrongs
inflicted by his words.

I contemplated
his imposture
while others pretended
not to notice his deceit.

As a wasp in the nest,
he turned me out
on the street
where I hid
in plain sight.

I flinched
when their eyes
sauntered slowly
over painted skin.

Fear surfaced
through the passages
that traced the rosy rings
on the sleeves of my shirt.

To escape,
I forgot about my past.

Smelled the moisture
of the seep
that dripped in the pool
at the back of the cave.

I surfaced
through the finest clay
in the image of the Goddess,
looked into her eyes

And then I ran.

And as I fled,
I invented a façade
that presented my unconscious
as framed by my essence
and I made a solemn vow
of devotion to my Self.

A Walking Naked Dream

You ring the bell.
There is no answer
at the gate.

They'd rather
not bother
but will linger
in the habits
of a lifetime.
Why try so hard
to reach them.

You say
they are jealous.
Competing to win
but I'm scared
to be wrong.

A nervous habit
long imposed
with robes of black
and a bib of white
and a scarf
to cover her hair.

A uniform of sameness
complete with a mask.

They can't see my smile
So I don't have to
appease
or try so hard to please.
I'm easy prey
to a silver-tongued con
I grew up fast and alone.

Tarnish turned me cynical.
I don this shielding armor
to keep from being seen,
though that is what I really want.

I hear them welcome me
into the conspiracies.
I don't fit in, I never fit in.
Even as I try
a chameleon dress
I am found out.

I wander lacking worthiness,
I've been drinking deep
from the cup
of self-loathing.

Instead of acceptance
I can't shake the belief
that I don't measure up
like a bad dream
where my shirt is inside out
and I'm walking
naked in the street
and I can't wake up.

There are no stories
with parables
or fantasy friends
who hold the key
to open my heart.
I'm locked deep inside
seeking perfection
in my imagination.

❖

Unbind My Wrists

I must release
The thoughts that swarm
In tiny threads inside my mind

A swirling cloud of calling crows
They spiral down
into the depths of foggy muck
I cannot breathe

I suffocate and cannot call
My voice is locked
Within a vice

A cage of wire
entwines my throat
To stop the words
from getting out
I must remake this life I live

I follow threads
from woven nests
I hear beliefs
persuade and tell

They call like crows
and draw me in
Their rigid thoughts
I take as mine
My echoed calls
reflect them back
I am not them

I write my truth
the threads unwind
The spirals twist
to clear my mind

Where secret fears
Are held inside a wire cage
I raise my arms
unbind my wrists
And take the pen

To find release
I bleed them out
Unleash my thoughts
I speak my truth
In single drops

Notes:

Surrender

Nature's Quiet Logic

Elements abstracted
from the math of things
belong to the earth.

The trees speak with reason
absent any formal thought.

Your soul's impulse
embraces your Divine.

She sees the order
In the wordless stories
of the field,
where flowers
kissed by bees
reflect the joy
of the mating dance.

Standing in the glitter
of the moonwake
elemental dancers
wander through
a secret existence.

Their repeated spiraling
pulses out a requiem
that instructs us
in the cycle of logic
found in nature.

The science of the form
Is reflected in the arc of the sun
across the sky.

Trees whisper secrets
in their leaves.
Softness left in droplets
blankets the unrelenting noise.

There is no such thing
as one way liberation
when you drop inside and
surrender to reality.

❖

Of Finger Ships

Each footprint
marks my track
as I step
into moist air
open spirit to sky
inhale blue
and exhale shades of grey.

The mountains hold
the rain to come.
The trees lean in.

Anticipate
the coming wind.
Leaves surf in circles,
then settle gently
nesting on the earth.

Each day
brings new adventure
with the unexpected wind.
A bell sounds
at the iron gate
and a visitor drops their stone.

Each voyage
brings expansion of
the conversation with ourselves.

We make an
election of decision,
with deliberate intention;
an act of rebellion for some.

Others use distraction
to set aside their chat.
Each selection,
adds to the collection.
A shoulder bag, worn thin,
shoes with long green laces
and tokens
to ease my passage,
through the shallows,
where the fish arrive
to greet my finger ships.

As they taste the tips
I search the
disembarking crowd,
for glimpses of myself.

Releasing Time

We willingly connect our lives
to beveled gears that move in sync.
They keep precisely measured time.
A counted life, allotments made.

We dedicate a plan to change
and focus on performance tasks
to push toward our ordered goal.

And in a slow and stately dance
a minuet of formal steps
designed to cross the finish line.
Slow motion as we break the tape.

When we finally make the shift
within a second truth's revealed.
We split the instant into two:
anticipation of before and
pleasure as the line is crossed.

We sit within a changeless state.
Within this holy moment lies
escape from measurement of guilt.
Remembering eternity
at last there is a space for peace.

❖

Suspended in the Moment

Sometimes
an urgent need
rises from
beneath your skin.

The prickling sensation
awakens you at moonrise
propels you from your bed
and walks you across
the cool moist sand
down wooden planks
to the end of the dock
where you
step off.

Suspended
in the moment
between dropping
and rising to the surface
you make your choice.

❖

Tendrils of Uncertainty

A surety of black and white
observes it all with sharpened eyes
that narrow in their judgment.

With urgency, assessments made
slicing and arranging
according to the formula
knowing they are right.

An uncertainty of smoke
brings a mercury of shades
of shifting, drifting points of view.
It stands in many shoes.

A varietal of tastes
brings a shift in realization
and the light of possibility
reveals a truth.

The uncertainty takes root.
Its tendrils slide beneath the door
and slip into the cracks.

Not knowing
is a seething rise of bile:
a clenching of denial
that turns its face away
as faith appears
with a side-eyed look
and throws the windows wide.

Then standing in the gale
I step toward the fear
and breathe.

Allowance is an opening.
The body is a sensing field
receiving each impression
then the letting go releases them.

I gently slide the feelers out
and cast into the burbling stream
where each stone sounds a different note
a flight of liquid magic brings
expansion in a drift of mist.

❖

A Pausing Time

When observing
from a distance
through the mist
of grey and green
you see when
something changes.

A shifting in the trail
is a pivot in your pathway
there is a pausing time
to consider your choices,
and ponder the direction
of your life.

You can make an election.
A conscious decision.
Like choosing shoes
with heels to match
a special dress.

Or choosing army boots
with metal studs
and buckles

black with zippers
up the sides.
Because it feels right
in that moment
when you
pause.

But instead
you bow your head
and close your eyes
and blindly let it go.
Tumble in the changing wind
slide like quicksilver
along the path of fate.

You choose not to choose.
And by this
You make a choice.

❖

A Butterfly Song

If a butterfly could sing
would it breathe a song of fluttering
and the lift of soft warm breezes.

A gentle strumming
on the strings of a harp
soft as a whisper
of tales of fields
of ringing bells of blue;
golden nectar within.

Would it sing of change
and the light of spring;
or a country song
of sunshine in the tall grass.

Or of the kisses of a daisy
light as the touch
of a summer bee
in the meadow,
where sunrise markers drift
in the realm of seeds.

Would it sing of sacrifice,
striking swift as a dragonfly,
in an aerial war
zipping along
on the surface of the pond.

An aria of trilling
notes complexity within
the turning of the wheel.

Suspended in a moment
where endings are beginnings
we are all in the sacrifice zone.

❖

Search For Peace Of Mind

I duck my head
in cool swift water
and surface gasping
at the momentary distraction.

We jump off the bridge
like trout that leap
to rid themselves
of parasites.

I try to ease
my worried mind
as bits and pieces
float away
drifting in the current.

I search for peace of mind
along the rocky shore,
turning over every stone
seeking some relief.

All I find are crabs
that grasp and pinch
and pull me down
until we level off.

I seek wisdom,
as I listen to the silence.
Trees send soothing tendrils
into air that's thick
with moss and mist.

I trace a pattern
on the map
along the ridges in the bark
yet cannot read the trail.

I climb higher
in the forest canopy
to see the bigger picture.
The air is thin and cold.

Tiny berries beckon.
I eat them as I pick.
They burst like sunshine
in my mouth.

Sensation pulls me back.

❖

The Passage

A Percussive Surfacing

Sharpening the edge,
we turn to tools
of practicality,
to hone the skills
no longer taught.

A mindset of
exclusion
prevents us
from becoming one.

Stories told
are handed down
as truth is locked
in mystery
and in myth.

This was a time
of boundless art
and the arousal
of thoughts.

They bring
an awakening
of sound
that brings healing
to our hearts.

❖

Time to Consecrate the Wheel

We come upon the turning now.
It's time to consecrate the wheel
It spins the drifts of whirling dust
that swirl beyond our certain paths.

Perspective shifts as thoughts evolve
we waken with expanding eyes
like hinges on a rusty gate
unopened all these centuries past.

The truth reveals an inside voice
that orients your every thought.
Arrangements of mythology
deployed within your every act.

Beliefs held close to keep you safe
within the castle walls you built
upon the mountain of debris
collected from the stories told.

Drawbridge down, the gates rolled up
a world outside the stacks of stone.

Mirrors piled up at the foot
reflect convictions in your mind.

Take sweepings from the castle keep
and press them to extract the juice
begin to feed the souls that search
for healing truth in memories deep.

Allow each person's energy
to sense the texture of the walls
to find their heart beneath the stones
and touch aliveness for themselves.

If it fills your heart with joy
and lightness gives your spirit ease
then lean into your soul's desire
and take the actions that will please.

But when it starts to weigh you down
just let it drop onto the ground
then look to see which choice will give
the most aliveness in your life.

❖

Forgive

I carried packages of hate.
White hot bundles.
Anger tightly wrapped
with many lengths of twisted twine.
I held this burden close
unwrapped it often
and examined every reason.
I remembered well.

Justify.

I held each piece of blackened stone
and sharpened glass.
Turned them over, one by one,
and deftly honed their edges.
I invoked a recollection,
the close intense examination
that reveals the pain.

Savor.

I recalled the wrongs
and sliced open half healed wounds.
I swam deeply in the seething pool
and swallowed daily doses
of reminders and remembering
choking on the bitterness.
My inoculation,
a ward against hope,
on guard against love.
It shut me down.

Lock.

I dreamed a revelation,
of wasted years obsessing,
crippled by the sour bile of my choosing.
A change from righteous fever
of angry justification.
It brought imagination,
a new consideration,
another way to be.

Reveal.

49

I walked my weary bundles
down a different path
I held the wounded parts of me with gentle hands,
gasping at the tender touch I had withheld.

I sipped a soothing liquid
that quenched the blackened vessel of my heart.
Summoning the light, I breathed intention.
I held it in my mouth, as a treasure,
a small smooth stone that was a word.

Forgive.

❖

Lying is a Practiced Art

Lying is
a practiced art:
the habits ingrained
in their youth.

Some
were programmed
to deceive,
deny the truth
to keep them safe.

Their grand illusions
illustrate
a perfect state
of stasis held.

Where balanced scales
are held above
as evidence
of virtue kept
and promises
of safety nets.

Some
will lie
to keep them where
delusions float
their reality.

They climb the ride
deception brings
where our emotions
have no place.

Where shame will drive
illusions deep
and feed us truth
of wrongness told.

I pick them up
and pack them deep
til I'm convinced
these views are mine.

Until I hear
the messages
that bring me words

to break the spell,
invite a
vulnerability
that helps to change
my point of view.

Mythology
protects my mind:
they can't convince me
lies are true.

And when my questions
make a shift
the veil lifts from
the camouflage
revealing how
they used our thoughts
to protect
their woeful tale.

We pull the rubber
band and feel
it sharply snap
back into place.

And when we see
the broken spells
reality does not exist.

A change that's forced
will never last,
but when illusion
circles round
perspective shifts
and spirit wins.

There be Dragons

At the end of the course
that was set for your ship
and you sail to the point
where the edges are,

Will you tumble into
unknown lands
that are marked
with a resinous
dragon's blood.

When you reach that point
of no return
where the victors drew
the lines on the map,

And the borders are laced
with fields of mines
in the no man's land
of unclaimed space,

Do your sentinels watch
the tendrils breach
the walls set alight
by a serpent's breath.

Will the embers burning
in your heart
take time to check
the boundary set?

When they cross that line
and trip the wire
do you lean in
or step away?

❖

Witnessing the Truth

We witness stories
as repeated chanted sound
that cloaks us with protective webs
to cover our indifference.

Deep within our memory
we find recited texts
that reinforce
our illusions of belief.

We maintain a conformity
and pacify capacity
for endless indecisions
that justify
and duplicate
our actions for our self.

Our stories keep
our views the same
while our perspective shifts,
until we find the subtle match.

We explore the evidence
and search for proof of facts
that build the case
to demonstrate a truth

that we believe with certainty
is always absolute.

Forget the possibilities.

Resist consideration
of any shift in view
that opens up a universe
where altered potential
presents a smorgasbord
of choice.

Instead, inscribe it deeply
onto a tattered map
of mediocre offerings
to guide half hearted promises
to live a mundane life.

Create a destination
where sneaky thoughts
direct our view
toward the tinted glass
when the patterns are the proof.

We see the puzzle fit our view
of life above the boards
disregarding what we hide
beneath.

Our testimony shapes our world
as we dispute the score
instead of asking what it is
we withhold from our dreams.

But when we choose facility
to expand capacity,
it sparks us out of latency,
examining our grace.

It walks us through
the passageway,
by showing what is viable,
not searching for the proof.

❖

Wu Wei

To surrender to our fears
Is to choose
a different path.

Where once there was
a certain track
doubt slips down
between the cracks

and we are slowly
threaded through
a minefield full
of musts and should

Where trepidation
dogs our steps
our inner whisper
goes unheard
by our deaf
and faithless ears.

Their expectations
shift our task
toward the place
where duty serves

and we are bound
to follow through.

The way toward
totality
is streaming through
the channeled route

and tumbling down
the rounded rocks.
The water always
finds its way.

And as the striders
zip along
the tension of the
surface breaks.

And fear dissolves
in widening rings
and near the shore
a songbird sings.

❖

Fifth Month Darkness

The evening burns
with the afterglow of day
as the fifth month darkness
closes like a curtain call
and we sit in folding chairs
gazing at the theatre in the sky.

We watch the stars appear.
They are longing for connection,
illuminating
what is held inside.

As their light
trickles through our heads
we feel the friendship
of ancient souls.

Darkness pulls
the strings that trail
beneath your heart.

The vastness gives permission
to the deepest yearnings
lurking at the frontier
of healing and desire.

Will you lend your mind
to attend to your fingers
as they quietly stroke
the tempered glass?

Do you see the patterns
reflected back at you?
Are you distracted by events
and complicated questions
that beg for answers
only listening can solve?

Be present in your life.
Our minds are replaced
by a semblance of ourselves.

We are magnified in multiples,
imprisoned by our wants.
Overwhelmed by numbers,
we seek freedom from the noise.

The deepest connection
on this edge of totality
is found behind
our veil of differences.

❖

Searching For Solutions

Now the days are flying by
the Ides have come and gone.
Tidal waves are crashing on
the beaches of our hearts.

A change in perspective:
brought a realization
as we suddenly awakened
to the starkness of the truth.

We are standing our ground
by anchoring in density
so we can find stability.
By widening our stance
there's a way to stay upright.

Now we play the longer game.

It's a re-imagination
of the need for a transition.
A remaking of our lives.
New patterns are emerging
in our social distanced lives.

As we rally for the changes
there's a need for new creation
and some thoughtful reflections
on the pieces of our world.

There's the tension of the 'needing'
and a sense of 'fully giving'
that brings me to the depths
of a deepening exhaustion.

We've been searching for relief
in the middle of a slowdown,
while the rising of anxiety
brings a fire to our belly
that burns inside our bones.

Within the isolation
we are weaving ways to gather
in collective intersections
finding balance in the gathering,
and the need to bring the fight.

We are caught in reimagining
all the ways to be a human

with a greater recognition
of a past preoccupation with
a focus on our selves.

And it brings a recognition
of our need to work together
toward an evolution
within collaboration.
where we search for revolution.

We are fighting for our lives.

❖

The Spinning of the Coin

The coin is spinning on the plate
both sides reflect the silver light.
And when you choose to yield to trust
the core of soul is filled with faith.

It overflows with seven gifts
fulfilling what the maiden spoke.
as she received the signs of birth
to wash in salt and consecrate.

But then a choking of the path
will bring you to the edge of fate.
You draw the sword that shimmers blue
to recreate defensive spells.

It pierces through the light of day
that clearly writes the passage here.
To guide you through the obstacle
there is no fear remaining there.

Now abundance calls to you
it glows beyond the garden gate.

Around her neck a key is held
she will reveal the gifts within.

But if you choose to linger in
the garden filled with all your dreams
you risk the languor of the wealth
and might be hiding from your fear.

Arise and take the hardest step
to love that is beyond the walls.
Go find your truth outside the gate
You have the key, the world awaits.

Forgive, Don't Forget

Forgetting
is

a state of mind
all solutions sought:
remembrance required.

Eventually,
I make a choice;

A random selection
to leave a part of life behind,
discarded, like worn out shoes
that traveled far
and took you to places
that you no longer
want to visit.

Forgetting
is

an act of courage
that releases thoughts.
It's a conscious letting go
to leave a habit behind.

No excuse to keep you here
or hold you from the open road
or places where you feel the pull.

Fresh adventures taste better
than grey stale crackers
from the opened box.

Forgetting
is

a reflexive flinch;
a switch turned off.
No decision needed
no worries, you say.

While all the while
you scream inside
stuffing memories
too painful to unveil.

Forgetting
is

a wiping out
with full consent
or something taught
on second thought

A mindset
that obscures the facts
that might have been
a lesson learned.

Unless you make
the choice to see
you cannot shine the light
to reveal them to your heart.

Forgive
don't forget

❖

The Rituals

We Swallow Light

Beneath The Forest Floor

Forests fill with jazzy notes
and then with mournful wailing blues
as booming dirges echo through
the deepness of their roots beneath.

Dendrites of the forest brain
extend their slender tendril's reach.
Their feelings transfer
through these nerves
electric pulses snap and surge.

I tip the bucket on the earth
the peelings slide into the pile
where grains of coffee spill like seed
as corn husk papers rustle skirts.

I see the strings of angel hair,
they mix with ashes from the stove
as stardust softly slips inside
mingling with mold and lime.

They warm the feet of forest trees
in holy mounds that give the roots
the nutrients that grow them tall
so they can meet their destiny.

Inhaling brings a memory
of childhood visits to the farm,
where chocolate with a hint of pipe
and sawdust sang a melody.

The complex notes a symphony
of musk and dusk and smoky moss.
We will bring that treasure here
as offering to the forest gods.

Stories in Ashes

The memories held within her bones
were set there by a spirit god.
Dense fibers seeped in liquid souls
and mingled in the marrow held.

She eats their ash to hear the songs,
and sips from chalice skulls to know.
For only they remember all
the tales and lives of ancient roots.

The singer moves within the bones,
to rows of skulls, each one a verse.
She sees them there and picks one up
It tastes of blood and promises.

She feels the tale and starts to sing,
of jeweled beasts and craggy keeps
With gardens full and lush with fruit
and daughters blushing in their silks.

The legends tell of feuds and deaths,
of love fulfilled that caused the wars.

Each story has a teaching thread,
that winds around a wooden spool
And thus reveals the warp and weft
to draw the part that isn't said.

With both hands raised, she tells the tales
a finger game that marks the lines.
Then stamps her feet to mark the course.
Her wisdom lives within the dance.

❖

The Blessing Tastes of Lost Promises

Remember where the crosses are.
They mark the sites of suffering
It helps us find the frozen souls
who witnessed the encircling.

Wide awake yet deeply felt
with light, we draw the symmetry
between the lines and lies we laid,
the air and lives that make our place.

Until consideration starts
a search for meaning deep within.
and all the rings that must be blessed
forever binds us to this place.

A golden sunset never formed
as ticking seconds seem like hours.
When holding secrets carried close
we reconcile the sacred pact.

The Hour of Cowdust

Walk your lines with care:
Gently brush the ground.

Settle your feet softly
one by one.
Fill each step
with focused breath.
Whispered invocations,
tracing cords of service.
Each footfall measures grace.

Wear moccasins, soft and brown
with flowers laced with beads.
A primal dance of oneness with the earth.
Take them off
and shuffle through the leaves.
The red dust hardens your soles.
We call them summer feet.
The spring invokes the rite
of toughening:
In fall we race down any trail.

Wear your kick ass boots;
a sassy way to trace the course.
A change of pace: a stronger gait:
the spirals deeper now,
more clear.
Suspended in the moment,
I find my voice;
I declare my boundaries.

Wear your rituals near your heart.
Practice every day.
In faith, I mark my way
with order and with words.
I breathe in grace and light
circling inward on the path
until I reach my center.
Then I circle out again.

Walk on forest trails
in silence,
snaking through the woods
along the path to reach the sea
and when you circle back again
it's with a lighter heart.

When we next meet
at the hour of cowdust,
We'll walk in grooves
worn in the earth;
And when our time
together ends
I'll slowly walk away.

❖

The Mind Collage

We gather golden fragments.
Collect the pieces of thoughts
made of rough-hewn wood
and polished stone.

Words inscribed on papers
made of leaves.
Arranged
so they speak to you
in whispers softly through
the layers intertwined.

Colors combine.
They build a new reality
that spirals in
to the center of meaning.

Creating the whole
out of pieces
you collected
from the musings
of your mind.

The Watcher Emerges

The circular sail
sweeps around the sun
revolving to reveal
the shelter of the watching one.

She extends
her leathered wings
their veins and pleats
flare open wide.

Strings of dander
woven in mesh
are drawn along
the thinly feathered spines.

Her eyes flick wide
at movement
on the edges of the world
where stillness is required.

Her mind reaches out
to grasp the offending ship.

She binds it tightly
in a web of circuitry.

A blinding light performs the rite
combining all to one.
The fiery blast,
her sole diversion in the field.

The task complete
she stretches her wings.
They accordion
then billow into place.

The others sealed
in chrysalides
sleep in graves
of blackened stone.

Patience waits
the turning of the wheel
to split the shells enclosing them.

Settling in
the watcher waits.

The Circle Brings Eudaimonia

Sentinels watch
my approach
from within
the forest deep.

I am surrounded
by consoling souls,
connected
to their guidance.

The trees
are touchstones
marking my trail
to the center
where the opening
exists.

A spiral set in stones
marks the path
meandering
on a journey
to the altar.

I bring the sacred books
as an offering.
Lay them to eternal rest
with memories of the wise.

A murmured blessing
brings the power
of the encircled ones
as they intersect
with the divine.

Their words live
in the earth,
tapped by the trees
I hear them later
as they echo in the wind.

❖

The Connection Burns

The coils
of our connection
closely wrapped
peel my
emotions raw.

The circuit opens.

Charged
by the current
I become the conduit
holding a live wire
unable,
to open my hand
and let it go.

The spark runs
through me
burning out
the softness in my heart
until it exits
through charred soles.

The grass afire,
the meadow burning black
as the forest ignites
feeling fear in fireballs
leaping
through the tops of trees.

I am renewed.

❖

I Will Not Blush For Death

When it arrives,
I will not blush for death
or bend my head in fear.
My hands will light a fire instead;
ignite the blaze upon the pyre.

Then rising from my burning bed
I will stand engulfed in flames
that consecrate my very blood
until I rise in swaying bands
of color dancing in the north.

A shooting star will mark the trail
where I will whisper in the void
the tales that penetrate your bones
our ancient roots and songs and spells.

And when my light has left your eyes,
then you will fall upon your knees
in honor of the gift bestowed
of blood and family secrets told

The Whisperer

It takes time
to warm up
like tubes in an old radio
the receiver tuned to messages
coming from your heart.

The crystals crackle
like a live wire
in the ghost filled attic
of my mind
as I try to dial it in.

Voices behind
our veil of differences
bring a whisperer
that mingles with our silence
to pursue the hope that sits
within my words.

I seek knowledge
but the answer
startles me.
I am forced to dig deep

to find a way
to admit
the light of understanding.

To defeat the shadow
smothered in
someone else's photo,
I reject the picture as presented
and choose the frame
that reconciles the sacred
and activates my love.

When I am restless
in my clarity
I bind it in a vow
tied in a ribbon of words.

As darkness lifts a glass
I drink the elixir
of forgiveness
in toast to your purity
that shines like a lamp
within a jar.

Meadow Dancers

Heavy clouds reflect
the luster of the rising sun.
It drips a liquid gold
into the river near the field.

The trail of light is followed
by the turning face of every leaf.
They stretch in yearning for its touch
as wildflowers shed
their downy mantles of the night.

They spread their dancing skirts
in a flowing ring, waiting to receive.

When the essence intermingles
with the kernel of the seed within,
they release the dust of all they hold
as an earthy starlit trace
of infinity in their wake.

❖

We Swallow Light

The bottoms of my feet
sing the light that
in a liquid feed of juice
that trails from fingertips
as tracer lines that track
the stars that move
across the vault.

I am infused with wonder.
Gazing at the glowing sky
the starlight fills my eyes
in alternating currents
like a steady flow of fireworks.
A circle flares and snaps
the arc flash triggers
an explosion with emotive force.

Each beginning is a thought.
A small shared intention
released into the air
fusing a connection
where our minds expand
in exponential strength

to conduct the power
of the circled ones.

A gathering of choice
reveals intention that
generates the spark.
The flames expand
and circle back.
The pulling ebbs and flows
as it never has before.

We swallow light.
Renew the source.
As we run our potency
its desire converts us all.

Within the heady atmosphere
an overload of will exerts.
As particles fly outward
stacked rings streak away.
The energy accelerates
a wave of echoed sound and source.

Positively charged air
tastes of toast and dust
as it caresses skin
I draw it to my chest
and wire it to the earth
where it grounds the source
and stores it in our hearts.

❖

Moving Through The Storm

Hover me close
to the center
of the hurricane.

The eye of the storm
shelters me
as destruction passes
and the deep question
is about choice.

Lurking underneath
is a yearning fire
of receiving
recognition.

The background
holds excitement
as emotions are reflected
in clear pools below.

The earth glows
in the summer sun

of our well being
and the sixes of the three
overcome the challenge.

Eventful twins
of judgment and forgiveness
reflect in our hearts
the deepest truth
is strength and health.

An attitude brings
the heat of discontent
as a bright awareness
of innocence and knowledge
rises in my consciousness.

The moment of choice
is suspended on an ideal,
as it dangles
over insecurity
as a decision
of direction
brings community
to an end.

Notes:

Choosing Love

Painting with Breath

I dreamed of flying
each breath released a gentle sigh
as gossamer wings lift
in surrender to the summer breeze.
I blinked and held a brush,
a long, black wand,
the tip as soft as eyelashes.

My arm breathes color
as an image drifts into the space.
A shape rises to the surface
through the fog and mist.

You appear in sacred form
and say
fly with me.

Hearth and Heart

The ritual begins
with the lighting
of the fire.

She clears her mind,
opens the book
and reads an invocation
to begin the day.

Holding the light,
she circles the room,
weaving protections
to prepare the space.

She honors spirits
and blesses the portals
with gestures
entrusted by the blood
of the family lines.

Tasks performed
with focused intention
bring the power in
as the master of the secrets.

She holds the heart
of the hearth
in the hollow
of her palm.

The energy infuses
all that enter here.

❖

I Feel Your Whispers on My Skin

Surrounded by
a whiff of petrichor,
the freshness of the
outdoor air
lingers on your shirt.

I feel your solid warmth
as you hold me close
and I smell you on my skin
as it holds a residue
of the summer wind.

I see you in my skin.
My lonely heart
holds the memories
in the membranes
of our love.

I see you in
the water spray.
My paddle flicks
the stream into the lake.

I see you as I lift my cup
with trembling hands
and trace the tiny roses
of the pattern painted there.
We toasted to our love
dipping for the liquid
from the depths
of the stream.

I dial you in and
hear you in the song.
Your notes descend
in minor keys
where they become
forever
a condition
of my heart.

I see you in our footsteps
as I trace them with my own.
When I see her face,
you are living in
the corner of her smile.

I inhale the dust of you
in the pages of my book.
A piano softly plays.
Secrets of infinity
sit inside the songs.

Notes repeating softly,
fall from my fingertips
like a waterfall
echoing the end of love.

I Trace A Path

We walk in moss
Breathe in thick grey fog
And sink in depths
Of soft moist earth.

Its pungent mix
Of death and life
It smells of wind
And ocean spray.

With stars at night
Outside of time
We walk transfixed
Until we wake.

And dance at dawn
To bring the light
We live our lives
An easy pace.

I trace a path
Between the leaves

Within the earth
I blaze the trees.

The breadcrumbs leave
your fingertips
as teardrops fall
upon your lips.

❖

Make Magic by Changing Direction

Stones rattle in his pockets.
Stars shimmer in his eyes
as he makes his weary way.

A promise to future chances.
Never to regret
the choosing
of his own winding path

Leaping high.
Heart in the glittering
moonlight.
He's going to travel far.

Work the dark shift,
sleep the daylight away.
Pebbles held
gently in his mouth
taste like nickels.

They set the stage
and seek the magic.
Making his own
by changing direction.
The heart shows the way.

❖

Ode to the Sun God

In the stillness of the night
she tucks her head beneath her wing
and makes herself a bit of fluff
deep in the hollow crack between
a fence post and a cedar stump.

The nightingale looks at the sky
where leaves are twirling in the wind.
They settle softly in the moss
a blanket for the forest god.

She rustles in her solitude
and whispers softly to herself
the colors of the harmonies
a song she holds inside her throat.

She tests the trills and longer notes
that roll within the complex tune
so smooth and fresh the liquid sounds
like sap that rushes in the trees.

When early twilight brushes
she stretches out her small brown wings
and standing tall upon the post
she pours her throat out to the sun.

❖

Line Dried Sheets

I want to dance
through flowered meadows in the spring
to turn my face to touch the shining wind
as rain brings freshness to the air.

I want to feel the fields
reach toward returning geese
and hear them greet familiar lands
where young fish rise in shallow pools
and birdsong rises to the clouds.

I want to smell the cottonwood,
to see its drifts of summer white
as plumes of seeds release and
seek a moist nest in the earth.

I want to chase a cloud of fireflies
running in my garden boots
as I catch them in my net
and save them in my fairy jar
to watch them twinkle in the night.

I want lightness in my breath
my feet to sweep through fallen leaves
that swirl in circles settling on
the carpet of the forest floor
and a bounce in my step
until the half years end.

I want to gently hold
your hand in mine,
to skip through snowflakes
as the moonlight
floats through streetlights
and the winter withering
brings closure to the year.

I want to carry you as treasure
clearly in my mind.
Each moment I've collected
is a jewel I hold up to my eyes
as a prism made of memories.

I want to hold the sky
forever in my sight
the oceans green and blue

all hues and tones
the depth of light
and height of darkness
and always
to see your eyes smile.

I want birdsong at sunrise
their humming fills my ears
with cool smooth songs that speak
and seek the ocean depths.

The piercing eagle cry
as it calls to its mate
and the sound of your voice
the deep heat of your breath
speaking words of love.

I want stillness
and peace
and line-dried sheets.

Soft down blankets
to wrap us close
and hold us safe
and in our arms
there is love
until the end of things.

We Walk Into The Bliss

My mind drifts.

Thoughts disperse in tiny cuts
as the whip licks its lips.

Memories break away
in large grey chunks of ice
and crash into the sea
sinking out of sight.

I lose the marks and blazes on the path
and mourn their loss.
I wonder why I throw my tears
against the wailing wall.

Demons drink their tea
while curling in my ears.
They leave a swirling trail
of leaves in the bottom of my cup.
I cannot read them.

Cement is setting
on the furling sails of my ship.
I trace the patterns of the grains in hardened sand
until it falls between my fingers.
as I lose the trail again,

I do not know what course to set.

I am adrift.

You take my hand
and walk beside me as we track a memory past.
We wade through thoughts
that pull us off the path.

I stumble and you tighten your grip.
When we reach the clearing
where the sun
paints mottled patterns on the grass,
we pause
and then we walk
together into the bliss.

❖

Index of First Lines

Reader Reviews

I love your poems Tree! I am in love with nature as well and I am fascinated by the patterns that we see there! So amazing! Thank you for sharing!
Trista Signe Ainsworth

Absolutely beautiful. Your sensory art is so masterful. In these lyrical bounces, skillfully composed lovely stories take us to the vast field and to a cozy home. This is a kind of poem that I want to read again and again to cherish. Thank you Tree.
Kyomi O'Connor

There is something so calming and beautiful about line-dried sheets. :) beautiful. This poem is absolutely beautiful. The imagery is incredible.
Jennifer McDougall

Thanks for sharing this beautiful poem! I love the lyrical quality of the shifting visuals. I found myself pondering how much the focus is on the setting for love, leaving the character of the other dancer as almost a hint or a shadow.
Jonathan James Anderegg

Tree you are a wonderful poet. You connect to any subject.
Dr. Preeti Singh

Love this !!! LOVE THE FRESHNESS that's there in it.
Actually, love all your poetry Tree Langdon.
Stay blessed and keep inspiring us with your words.
Geetika Sethi

Your affinity with nature definitely has a positive effect on wellbeing. Your poem spoke to this with reverence and tenderness.
Carolyn Hastings

I love the prophetic tone of this, and how your truth comes out in single drops. Is each drop a poem?
Zachary Burres

Tree. This is so compelling. Beautiful. I am so glad I found it and read your striking words.
Suzanne V Tanner

I love the flow of this. It also feels like a dream.
This is one of my favs.
M.C. Commander

About This Book

It's your deepest fear
No one understands your pain
Could it be you'll always feel alone?

Maybe you've never read an honest poem.
Maybe no one has ever told you a story that touched
your heart.

This book is full of raw truths,
written by someone who understands what it's like
to try and fail.
...and then to fall and pick yourself up again.

Would you rather be lonely?
Or would you like to find a way to make a deep
connection?

With this series of poems, the author shares her
deepest fears
and shows you how you can move through your pain
to find a better life.

In 'A Walking Naked Dream,' she explores growing up
fast and alone.
Then her powerful words draw you into the poem
'Forgive' as she finds a way to leave her anger
behind. She did it and you can too.

About The Author

Tree Langdon, is a Canadian writer and artist.

A selection of her poems have been published in the anthology, _Breathing Words_.

She is a contributing member of the international online weekly, _Poem Kubili_ and _the Rebelle Society_.

Tree writes about personal failings, addiction, grace, the power of thought, and really whatever else she wants to.

If you loved this book, please write a review. It really helps other readers find her book.

Twitter: @treelangdon
Medium: @treelangdon
Substack: WordsInMotion

ONE LAST THING...

Thank you so much for reading this book. I poured my heart into it.

❖

Could you do me a favor? Please review this book on Amazon and/or Goodreads. Whether you thought it was great, terrible, or anywhere in between, I'd love to have your feedback.

❖

Reviews are the best way for an author like me to get discovered. Readers like you can help make it happen.

❖

Thanks in advance,

Tree Langdon